Why buying organic food is important.

Over hundreds of years, farmers and scientists have modified foods for their looks because people buy with their eyes. Fertilizers and pesticides have become normalized in the food industry and many people do not understand the effects these chemicals can have on the body. Glyphosate is a chemical used in roundup which is sprayed on many common crops such as wheat, oats, lentils, peas, soybeans, corn, flax, buckwheat, potatoes, sugar beets, potatoes, and more. This chemical can kill healthy gut bacteria, which disrupts the microbiome and can cause weight gain, disrupted blood glucose levels, high cholesterol, and metabolic problems. Along with the fact that organic foods are more nutrient dense and do not contain preservatives and pesticides, organic farming is better for the environment. Organic farming supports water preservation, prevents soil erosion, fights global warming, and does not use harmful pesticides that can leach into the environment. Many of my recipes in this book are vegetarian and vegan recipes because eating a plant based diet is not only beneficial to the environment, but it also gives your body a break from the process of digesting meat and dairy products which are more straining on the human body. I study environmental economics and management at Michigan State University, and I am passionate about the preservation of our planet and personal health. We only have one planet to live on, and we need to treat it with respect. The next time you go to the grocery store, think about what you buy. I understand organic food and plant based items can be more expensive, but the lasting impact of your choice can have benefits far beyond what you can see.

the cut

cookbook

Why are we called The Cut™?

In the 1800s, European Settlers attempted to connect Lake Leelanau and Lake Michigan in Northern Michigan. These settlers connected a trading dock to the property on Lake Michigan, and the dock's base still remains today. For years, by usage of horses and buggies, the locals worked to connect the two lakes. "The Sandcut" is the name the locals gave this piece of land. This project eventually came to a stop due to the fact that if the two lakes were connected, it would drain the much smaller Lake Leelanau. "The Sandcut" went on to be used by locals as a picnic hangout until the early 90's when a local bought "The Sandcut" and built a beautiful home. Thousands of people over several decades have lived out their own stories on this beautiful piece of land, me especially. "The Sandcut" holds a special place in my heart because it's where I created the book you're reading now. Not only is it a unique local historic landmark, but it provided me with the perfect name for my first cookbook, having written, designed, and photographed everything you see within these pages right here in "The Sandcut." I hope to bring attention to the treasured and historic piece of land that is now my home, as well as the great surrounding area of Leland.

Photographed in 1915

About The Author

Since a young age, one of my favorite places to be has been in the kitchen. I love any opportunity to be creative and was initially inspired by Buddy Valastro's "Cake Boss." Buddy had a way with desserts, and I credit his show for helping kickstart my food journey. At just ten years old, I began with an Instagram baking page full of eccentric desserts called @cake_cupcake_baker and have been playing in the kitchen ever since.

The only thing I love more than cooking and enjoying a great meal is watching other people get inspired and find joy through food. My friends at Michigan State University, where I'm currently studying Environmental Economics and Entrepreneurship, can attest to this. I've always been full of ideas when it comes to food. However, at the start of COVID-19, I was desperate for a creative outlet to help fill my time and serve as a therapeutic release. I decided cooking was much more than a hobby to me and began to compile all of my family and friends' favorite dishes so that I could share my love of cooking with others. My creativity has turned into reality with "The Cut Cookbook". It's been an incredible journey being able to see the recipes I've dreamed up at all hours of the day and night come to life on paper.

I hope that someday, The Cut™, filled with 100+ delicious eats, is a one-stop-shop for all your recipe needs. My goal is to help others have more fun and get comfortable expressing themselves in the kitchen, just like I have.

Buon Appetito!
Madison Marsh

Introduction

This cookbook is meant to be simplistic and straightforward. I want to encourage others to be more adventurous in the kitchen and try new things. This cookbook has been created and tested by me, my family, and close friends. I love to cook, but I am nowhere near a professional. Cooking is a social practice that brings people together. Food nurtures the mind, body, and soul, and that is why I love to cook. Whether you want simple comfort food, tasty gluten-free recipes, delicious healthy ideas, or easy-to-make recipes, my cookbook is made for you. Using clean ingredients and healthy organic foods is not only good for your body physically, but also good for your mind. When I cook food for myself and others, it makes me smile and it makes others smile, too. Do not be afraid to try new things, experiment with the recipes, and share the joy of cooking with others. I have also included a notes section on every recipe page so that you can make your own adjustments to the book. I hope this book will help you find a passion for cooking!

Favorite Buys & Tips

FAVORITE PRODUCTS

Oliviers & Co - Salt & Herb Mix for Pasta and Salad
Lakanto Maple Syrup
Golden Monk Fruit Sweetener
Ezekiel Bread
Julian Bakery Vanilla Granola
Garden of Life Vanilla Protein Powder
Primal Kitchen Avocado Oil Mayo
Miyoko's Vegan Butter
One Degree Organic Foods Sprouted Organic Oats
Kite Hill Unsweetened Almond Milk Yogurt
PB2 Organic Powdered Peanut Butter
Lily's Dark Chocolate Chips
Organic Coconut Butter
Siete Tortilla Chips
LesserEvil Popcorn
Mary's Gone Crackers Super Seed
Flatout flatbread
Pretzilla - Soft Pretzel Buns

COOKING TIPS

Always buy organic when possible.
Shop local.
Read the ingredients on the packaging.
The more raw foods the better.
Use services like Thrive Market.
Use healthy oils like avocado and olive.
A little oil goes a long way.
Adding texture to food can completely change the taste.
Dairy from animals other than cows is easier to digest.
Mixing salt, fat, acid, and heat creates a perfect meal.

Recipe List

breakfast

Blueberry Oatmeal

INGREDIENTS:
1/2 cup oats
1 tablespoon chia seeds
1 cup water
1/2 teaspoon cinnamon
1/4 teaspoon vanilla
1 teaspoon cocoa (optional)
1/4 cup blueberries

DIRECTIONS:
Add all ingredients to a sauce pan.
Bring mixture to a boil over medium
heat and stir occasionally. As the oats
cook, mash the blueberries with the
back of a spoon and stir. Once the
liquid has been absorbed by the oats,
transfer them to a serving bowl.
You can top your oats with more
blueberries, granola, and peanut
butter or honey.

Vegan Recipe

Cooking Time: 5 minutes

Serving Size: 1

Cooking Appliance: Stove

Notes:

Power
Oatmeal

INGREDIENTS:
1 egg (trust me)
1 cup water
1/4 cup oats
1 tablespoon chia seeds
1/2 teaspoon cinnamon
1/4 teaspoon vanilla

DIRECTIONS:
Whisk egg in a small bowl until smooth. Add remaining ingredients to a separate bowl and mix in the egg. Add the mixture to a sauce pan and cook on medium heat. Stir continuously so the egg does not separate. It will make the oats super fluffy! Cook for 3-5 minutes or until the oats have absorbed all the liquid. Transfer to a serving bowl and top with your fav fruits, nuts, coconut, honey, or a splash of milk.

Cooking Time: 5 minutes

Serving Size: 1

Cooking Appliance: Stove

Notes:

Birthday Cake Baked Oatmeal

INGREDIENTS:
3/4 cup water
1/2 cup oats
1/2 banana
1/4 cup egg whites
3 strawberries
2 tablespoons protein powder
1 teaspoon chia seeds
1/2 teaspoon baking powder

DIRECTIONS:
In a blender, add all of your ingredients and mix until the batter becomes smooth. Pour the batter into a microwave-safe bowl and heat for 5-7 minutes until the center becomes firm. Top with vanilla yogurt, sprinkles, and fruit. Enjoy!

Cooking Time: 5-7 Minutes

Serving Size: 1

Cooking Appliance: Microwave

Notes:

Lazy Morning Overnight Oats

INGREDIENTS:
1 cup nut milk
1/2 cup oats
1/4 cup berries of choice
2 tablespoons protein powder
    (optional)
1 tablespoon chopped walnuts or
    almonds
1/2 teaspoon cinnamon

DIRECTIONS:
Add all ingredients to a Mason jar.
Close the jar and shake to
combine.
Place the jar in the fridge and
let the oats sit overnight. In the
morning, enjoy on the go or add to
a bowl with your favorite toppings
and a little extra nut milk!

Cooking Time: 12 Hours

Serving Size: 1

Cooking Appliance: Fridge

Notes:

Super Chia Pudding

INGREDIENTS:
1 cup nut milk
1/2 cup coconut water
3 tablespoons chia seeds
1 tablespoon vanilla protein powder
1 tablespoon hemp seeds
1 tablespoon omega-3 fish oil
        (optional)
1 teaspoon vanilla
1 teaspoon spirulina
1/2 teaspoon cinnamon

DIRECTIONS:
Add all ingredients to a Mason jar and shake to combine. Let this sit for at least 3-5 hours in the refrigerator before enjoying. Shake jar occasionally to make sure the chia seeds are absorbing the liquid. Keep refrigerated.

Cooking Time: 3-5 Hours

Serving Size: 1

Cooking Appliance: Fridge

Notes:

Veggie Frittata

INGREDIENTS:
1/2 tablespoon olive oil
1/2 bell pepper, chopped
1/4 red onion, chopped
1/2 cup broccoli, chopped
1/4 teaspoon salt
1/4 teaspoon black pepper
1/4 teaspoon Italian seasoning
1/4 teaspoon paprika
1/2 cup spinach, chopped
2/3 cup egg whites
crumbled goat cheese
Frank's Red Hot Sauce

DIRECTIONS:
In a large skillet, add olive oil, bell pepper, broccoli, onion, salt, pepper, Italian seasoning, and paprika. Cook for 5-7 minutes, then add in the spinach. Cook for an additional minute, then add in the egg whites and cook for 3 minutes. Flip and cook for an additional 2 minutes. Move the frittata onto a plate, top with crumbled goat cheese and Frank's hot sauce, and enjoy!

Cooking Time: 10-12 Minutes

Serving Size: 2-4

Cooking Appliance: Stove

Notes:

Breakfast Burrito

INGREDIENTS:
1/4 bell pepper, sliced
1/4 red onion, sliced
4 baby mushrooms, sliced
1/4 teaspoon salt
1/4 teaspoon black pepper
1 teaspoon coconut oil
1/2 teaspoon paprika
1/4 teaspoon Lawry's Seasoned Salt
1/2 cup spinach, chopped
1/2 cup egg whites
1 tortilla
salsa verde

DIRECTIONS:
Prepare the vegetables in a medium skillet, add the oil, peppers, onions, mushrooms, and spices. Cook on medium heat for 10-12 minutes until the onions and peppers have softened. Then add your chopped spinach and sauté for 1 minute. Now add egg whites and cook for 3-5 minutes. Stir constantly to create a scramble. After this is complete, remove the scramble from the pan and place the mixutre on the tortilla. Fold your burrito, then add it back into the pan for 3-5 minutes to toast the tortilla. Serve with salsa verde and enjoy!

Cooking Time: 10-12 Minutes

Serving Size: 1

Cooking Appliance: Stove

Notes:

13

Breakfast Scramble

INGREDIENTS:
1/4 cup black beans
1/4 bell pepper, chopped
1/4 onion, chopped
1 handful spinach
2/3 cup egg whites

DIRECTIONS:
Prepare the Megan's 5-Minute Beans (see page 151). In a small skillet, sauté peppers and onions on high heat. Add in spinach and cook until it turns bright green. Add in cooked beans. Add in egg whites and scramble. Top with avocado and enjoy!

Cooking Time: 5-7 Minutes

Serving Size: 1

Cooking Appliance: Stove

Notes:

Breakfast
Hash

INGREDIENTS:
1/2 tablespoon avocado oil
1/2 bell pepper, chopped
1/4 onion, choppedl
2 breakfast sausage links, chopped
1/4 cup broccoli, chopped
1/2 teaspoon salt
1/8 teaspoon black pepper
1/4 teaspoon Italian seasoning
pinch of red chili flakes
1/2 cup chopped kale
1 cup water in a mug
1 egg
1 slice of toast
1/4 avocado

DIRECTIONS:
In a skillet on medium heat, add oil, bell pepper, onion, sausage, broccoli, salt, pepper, Italian seasoning, and red chili flakes. Cook for 5-7 minutes, then add in the kale, and sauté for 2 more minutes. Remove skillet from heat and set aside. While the vegetables are cooking, add 1 egg to a mug of water, and cook for 2 minutes in the microwave to make your poached egg. On the side, prepare the avocado toast (see page 51). Then add the vegetables to a plate, place the poached egg on top, and top with red chili flakes and enjoy!

Cooking Time: 9-12 Minutes

Serving Size: 1

Cooking Appliance: Stove & Microwave

Notes:

Sweet Potato Hashbrowns

INGREDIENTS:
2 sweet potatoes
Ice water
1/2 cup avocado oil
1 teaspoon black pepper
2 teaspoons salt
1 teaspoon paprika

DIRECTIONS:
First grate two sweet potatoes, add them into a bowl of ice water, and let soak for 15 minutes. Remove the potatoes from the ice water and dry thoroughly. In a large pan, add the oil and warm, over medium heat for 3 minutes. Then add the potatoes and spices and cook, stirring occasionally, for 15-20 minutes until the potatoes are golden brown and crispy. Remove the hash browns from the pan and immediately top with sea salt and enjoy!

Vegan Recipe

Cooking Time: 30-35 Minutes

Serving Size: 4-6

Cooking Appliance: Oven

Notes:

Banana
Pancakes

INGREDIENTS:
1 banana, mashed
1 egg
1/4 teaspoon baking powder
1/2 teaspoon vanilla
1/2 teaspoon cinnamon
2 tablespoons flax seeds
1 tablespoon oats
1 tablespoon almond flour
1 teaspoon coconut oil

DIRECTIONS:
Add all the ingredients to a bowl
and mix to combine. Heat a skillet
on medium heat with 1 teaspoon of
coconut oil. Add batter in heaping
tablespoons. Cover with a lid.
Flip pancakes once the batter
starts to bubble. Cook until both
sides are golden brown. Top the
pancakes with peanut butter,
almond butter, coconut, fruit,
honey, or maple syrup and enjoy!

Cooking Time: 5-7 Minutes

Serving Size: 2

Cooking Appliance: Stove

Notes:

Protein Pancakes

INGREDIENTS:
1/4 cup egg whites
1 scoop vanilla protein powder
1/2 teaspoon vanilla
1/2 teaspoon cinnamon
3 tablespoons nut milk
1/2 teaspoon baking powder
        cacao nibs (optional)
1 teaspoon of coconut oil

DIRECTIONS:
In a medium bowl, beat egg whites to stiff peaks. In another bowl, combine protein powder, vanilla, milk, cinnamon, and baking powder. Add more milk to the protein mixture if needed to make a thick batter consistency. Add 1/3 of the egg white mixture to batter and fold in gently until combined. Then fold, the remaining egg white mixture into the batter. It should be combined well and fluffy. Heat a skillet on medium heat with coconut oil. Add batter in heaping tablespoons and sprinkle with cacao nibs. Cover with a lid. Flip pancakes once the batter starts to bubble. Cook until both sides are golden brown. Top the pancakes with your favorite yogurt, fruit, nuts, honey, or maple syrup and enjoy!

Cooking Time: 5 Minutes

Serving Size: 2

Cooking Appliance: Stove

Notes:

23

Famous Flatout Roll

INGREDIENTS:
1 piece of original Flatout Flatbread
2 tablespoons peanut butter
1 tablespoon strawberry jelly
1 banana
3 strawberries sliced
2 tablespoons of granola

DIRECTIONS:
Spread peanut butter over one side of the entire Flatout then spread the strawberry jelly on top. Place the banana horizontal across the center of the Flatout and place the sliced strawberries along the banana. Finally sprinkle the granola on top of the Flatout then roll it up. Slice into 6 pieces and enjoy!

Cooking Time: 5 Minutes

Serving Size: 1

Cooking Appliance:

Notes:

25

Breakfast
Crunch Wrap

INGREDIENTS:
1 large tortilla
1/2 cup chopped spinach
1/4 cup egg whites
1/4 mashed avocado
1 sausage patty
2 tablespoons cheddar jack cheese

DIRECTIONS:
First place the chopped spinach in a small bowl and microwave for 30 seconds. Once the spinach is wilted add in the egg whites and microwave for 90 seconds. Cook the sausage patty as directed. Then layout the tortilla and spread the avocado in the center and place the sausage patty on top. Sprinkle 1 tablespoon of cheese on the sausage patty, then place the circular egg white patty on top, and add the other tablespoon of cheese on top. Then begin wrapping the tortilla. Take the tortilla and fold it into itself in five small triangles to seal the ingredients inside. Then place the folded side face down in a pan and cook for 2 mintutes, flip the wrap, and cook for 2 more minutes. Cut in half and enjoy!

Cooking Time: 5-6 Minutes

Serving Size: 1

Cooking Appliance: Microwave & Stove

Notes:

smoothies

Homemade Coconut Milk

INGREDIENTS:
2 tablespoons organic
coconut butter
3 1/2 cups water
2 tablespoons maple syrup
2 teaspoons vanilla
1 teaspoon cinnamon
1/2 teaspoon xanthum gum

DIRECTIONS:
Add all ingredients to a blender.
Blend till smooth.
Keep refrigerated.
Shake before using.

Vegan Recipe

Cooking Time: 5 Minutes

Serving Size: 4

Cooking Appliance: Blender

Notes:

Super Food Smoothie

INGREDIENTS:
1 scoop Garden of Life Raw Organic
        Meal Replacement Vanilla
1 teaspoon organic matcha powder
1 teaspoon organic turmeric
1 teaspoon organic açaí powder
1 teaspoon whole ground flax
1 tablespoon collagen powder
1 tablespoon Barlean's Omega-3
        fish oil, key lime pie flavor
1 cup coconut water
1/2 cup almond milk
1/2 cup blueberries
or strawberries
1/2 avocado
1 kiwi, peeled
1/2 banana
8 ice cubes

DIRECTIONS:
Put your liquid in the NutriBullet
or blender first, then add all other
ingredients and mix until smooth!

Cooking Time: 5 Minutes

Serving Size: 1

Cooking Appliance: Blender

Notes:

Tropical Smoothie

INGREDIENTS:
1/2 banana
1 large handful spinach or kale
6 chunks pineapple, 1-2"
2 tablespoons peanut butter powder
1/2 cup homemade coconut milk
1/2 cup coconut water
5 ice cubes

DIRECTIONS:
Add all the ingredients to a blender and mix until smooth. Enjoy in a glass, or a bowl with pineapple, coconut, and granola!

Cooking Time: 5 Minutes

Serving Size: 1

Cooking Appliance: Blender

Notes:

Perfect Smoothie

INGREDIENTS:
1/3 cup raspberries
1/3 cup mango
1/3 cup pineapple
1/2 cup coconut milk
1/2 cup coconut water
2 tablespoons vanilla protein powder
5 ice cubes
2 tablespoons of water
3 tablespoons of my super chia pudding (pg 9)
1 large handful spinach
1 tablespoon of avocado

DIRECTIONS:
Add all the ingredients to a blender and mix until smooth. Enjoy in a glass, or a bowl with bee pollen, coconut, or granola!

Cooking Time: 5 Minutes

Serving Size: 1

Cooking Appliance: Blender

Notes:

sandwiches
wraps & toasts

Bean & Chicken Quesadilla

INGREDIENTS:
1 large tortilla
1/4 cup goat cheddar
1/4 cup mozzarella
1/4 cup cooked pulled chicken
2 tablespoons Megan's black beans (see page 151)
2 tablespoons frozen corn, defrosted
1/8 red onion
1/4 teaspoon salt
1/4 teaspoon pepper
1/4 teaspoon red pepper flakes
1/4 teaspoon paprika
1 teaspoon avocado oil

DIRECTIONS:
Add your two cheeses to a bowl and toss with salt, pepper, red pepper flakes, and paprika. Then in a small pan add a splash of oil, corn, onions, and beans, sauté on medium heat until onions are golden brown. In a large skillet, add a small amount of oil, and place the tortilla in the pan. Add cheese, cooked chicken, and the corn and onion mixture to the tortilla. Place a lid on the pan, and cook for 3 minutes until the cheese begins to melt. Fold the tortilla over and press down on the quesadilla. Cook until both sides are golden brown, and the cheese has melted. Top with a little salt, pepper, salsa, and hot sauce. Cut into triangles and enjoy!

Cooking Time: 10-12 Minutes

Serving Size: 1

Cooking Appliance: Stove

Notes:

41

Black Bean Crunch Wrap

INGREDIENTS:
1 black bean burger
1 tablespoon avocado oil
1/4 avocado
5 pickled jalapeños, diced
2 tablespoons avocado mayo
1 tablespoon Frank's Red Hot Sauce
1 tortilla or egg wrap
shaved goat cheddar cheese

DIRECTIONS:
Prepare the sauce by combining the Frank's, mayo, and pickled jalapeños. Now in a small pan add the oil and let it warm up for 1-2 minutes. Then add your black bean burger to the pan and cook until golden brown. Remove from pan and add the tortilla or wrap to the pan. Spread a layer of sauce in the center of the tortilla and add the avocado then place the burger on top. Spread a second layer of sauce on top of the burger and add the shaved cheese. Fold the edges of the tortilla over the cheese and flip the wrap cheese side down. Cook both sides until golden brown, and enjoy!

Cooking Time: 10-12 Minutes

Serving Size: 1

Cooking Appliance: Stove

Notes:

Fancy Grilled Cheese

INGREDIENTS:
2 pieces bread, buttered
3 slices provolone cheese
2 slices prosciutto
fig jam

DIRECTIONS:
Spread a generous amount of fig jam on both slices of bread. Add 1 1/2 slices of cheese to each side along with the 2 slices of prosciutto. Place the bread together and butter the outside of both pieces of bread. Warm a skillet on medium heat, then add the sandwich, cover with a lid, until, the bottom is golden brown. Flip the sandwich and brown the other side. Cook until the cheese is melted. Place the sandwich on a plate, cut into triangles, and enjoy! Be sure to save the toasty pieces of cheese that melt. Those are the best!

Cooking Time: 5 Minutes

Serving Size: 1

Cooking Appliance: Stove

Notes:

Open-Face Tuna Melt

INGREDIENTS:
2 slices bread or an English muffin
1 can tuna
1 tablespoon avocado mayo
juice of 1/2 lemon
1/4 teaspoon salt
1/4 teaspoon pepper
1/2 teaspoon Lawry's Seasoned Salt
1 celery stalk, diced
2 pieces meunster or provolone
1/8 onion, diced
1 tablespoon of fresh basil, chopped

DIRECTIONS:
Drain one can of tuna and add it to a bowl. Add mayo, salt, pepper, basil, celery, onion, Lawry's, and lemon to the tuna. Mix until combined. Place your bread in the toaster until golden brown. Add the tuna to both slices of bread and place 1 slice of cheese on each toast. Place the toast in the microwave for 30 seconds or broil in the oven to melt the cheese on the top. Cut into triangles and enjoy.

Cooking Time: 5 Minutes

Serving Size: 1

Cooking Appliance: Toaster & Microwave

Notes:

Balsamic Pesto Toast

INGREDIENTS:
1 slice bread
1/4 cup sausage,
cooked and crumbled
1 tablespoon feta cheese
1 tablespoon pesto (see page 97)
balsamic glaze

DIRECTIONS:
First toast your bread in the toaster until golden brown. Now crumble the feta and cook the sausage and prepare the pesto. Once the toast is done, spread a generous layer of pesto onto the bread. Top with feta cheese, and then layer on the sausage. Cut the toast into triangles, drizzle with balsamic glaze, and enjoy.

Cooking Time: 10 Minutes

Serving Size: 1

Cooking Appliance: Toaster & Stove

Notes:

Simple Avocado Toast

INGREDIENTS:
1 slice bread
1 egg (optional)
1/2 tablespoon avocado oil
1/2 avocado
1/4 teaspoon red chili flakes
pickled onions (see page 169)
flaky sea salt
black pepper
olive oil

DIRECTIONS:
First, place the avocado oil in
a small pan and heat for
2 minutes. Then add egg and
cook to your satisfaction.
Place your bread in the toaster.
Set your egg aside and slice
1/2 avocado into thin strips.
Add the avocado to the bread.
Sprinkle salt and pepper onto
the avocado and add the egg
on top. Then layer the pickled
onions on top of the egg and
sprinkle with red chili flakes,
flaky sea salt, and a drizzle
of olive oil.

Vegan Recipe

Cooking Time: 5 Minutes

Serving Size: 1

Cooking Appliance: Stove & Toaster

Notes:

51

vegetable dishes

Roasted Acorn Squash

INGREDIENTS:
1 acorn squash
sprayable avocado oil
salt
black pepper
garlic salt

DIRECTIONS:
Preheat oven to 400° Fahrenheit. First cut your acorn squash horizontally in 1 inch strips. Then cut those strips in half leaving you with half circles. Next place your squash in an even layer on a sheet tray and spray one side with avocado oil. Then sprinkle a generous amount of salt, black pepper, and garlic salt over the squash. Flip your squash and repeat this on the other side. Place your sheet tray in the oven for 25-30 minutes, flipping the squash after 15 minutes. Then serve and enjoy!

Vegan Recipe

Cooking Time: 30 Minutes

Serving Size: 6-8

Cooking Appliance: Oven

Notes:

Mushrooms & Onions

INGREDIENTS:
2 cups mushrooms
1/2 red onion
1/4 teaspoon salt
1/4 teaspoon pepper
1 teaspoon olive oil

DIRECTIONS:
Slice the onions. Dice the mushrooms. Place the skillet on medium heat with the oil. Add the vegetables to the skillet with the salt and pepper. Then cook, stirring occasionally, for 7-10 minutes.

Vegan Recipe

Cooking Time: 7-10 Minutes

Serving Size: 6-8

Cooking Appliance: Stove

Notes:

Summer Roasted Asparagus

INGREDIENTS:
1 bunch asparagus
1/4 teaspoon salt
1/4 teaspoon garlic salt
1/4 teaspoon pepper
1/4 teaspoon Italian seasoning
1 tablespoon lemon olive oil

DIRECTIONS:
First prepare your asparagus by chopping two inches off the woody end. Then place asparagus in a bowl and toss with oil, salt, pepper, Italian seasoning, and garlic salt. Add these to a skillet or grill on medium heat and sauté until golden and crispy.

Vegan Recipe

Cooking Time: 5 Minutes

Serving Size: 4-6

Cooking Appliance: Stove or Grill

Notes:

Roasted Cauliflower with Pine Nuts

INGREDIENTS:
1 head of cauliflower
3 tablespoons pine nuts
3 tablespoons nutritional yeast
1/4 teaspoon salt
1/4 teaspoon pepper
1/4 teaspoon Italian seasoning
1-2 tablespoons avocado oil

DIRECTIONS:
Preheat oven to 400° Fahrenheit. Chop your cauliflower into small florets and place them on a sheet tray. Drizzle avocado oil over the cauliflower and mix until it is coated. Sprinkle your salt, pepper, and Italian seasoning over the cauliflower and mix. Top the cauliflower with the nutritional yeast and place in the oven. Let this cook for 25-30 minutes. Turn the cauliflower after 15 minutes. While the cauliflower is in the oven, place your pine nuts in a pan with salt and pepper and toast them over low heat until golden brown, stirring the pine nuts occasionally to prevent burning. When you reach the last 5 minutes of your cooking time, change the oven setting to broil and watch closely until the tops of the cauliflower begin to brown. Remove from the oven, top with your toasted pine nuts, and enjoy! Best served with a drizzle of balsamic glaze on top.
Vegan Recipe

Cooking Time: 25-30 Minutes

Serving Size: 6-8

Cooking Appliance: Oven & Stove

Notes:

Sweet Potato Fries

INGREDIENTS:
2 large sweet potatoes
2 tablespoons olive oil
1 teaspoon garlic salt
1 teaspoon salt
1/2 teaspoon pepper
1 teaspoon paprika

DIRECTIONS:
Preheat oven to 425° Fahrenheit.
Wash and slice the sweet potato
into thin long strips. Soak the sweet
potatoes in iced water for 20-30
minutes to release the starch.
Dry the potatoes and place them
on a baking sheet. Drizzle the oil,
garlic salt, pepper, paprika, and salt
over the sweet potatoes and mix.
Place in the oven for 25-30 minutes,
flipping the fries after 15 minutes.
Serve and enjoy!

Vegan Recipe

Cooking Time: 25-30 Minutes

Serving Size: 6-8

Cooking Appliance: Oven

Notes:

Broccoli Tater Tots

INGREDIENTS:
1/2 large onion, chopped
2 eggs
1/2 cup Pecorino Romano cheese
1/2 cup panko bread crumbs
1/2 cup gluten-free flour
2 cups whole broccoli
1/2 teaspoon Lawry's Seasoned Salt
1/2 teaspoon salt
1/2 teaspoon pepper
1/2 teaspoon Italian seasoning

DIRECTIONS:
Preheat oven to 425° Fahrenheit.
Roughly cut the broccoli before
adding it to a food processor
and blend into a fine crumb.
Add the remaining ingredients
to the food processor and mix
gently. Scoop into tablespoon-sized
balls and place on a parchment-
lined baking sheet.
Cook for 30 minutes, flipping
over the tots after 15 minutes.

Cooking Time: 30 Minutes

Serving Size: 4-6

Cooking Appliance: Oven

Notes:

Cauliflower Couscous

INGREDIENTS:
1/2 cup chopped dried apricots
1 large cauliflower head, roughly chopped
2 tablespoons olive oil
1 medium red onion, diced
2 cloves garlic, minced
3 cups spinach, chopped
15 oz can of chickpeas, drained
1/2 cup roasted pistachios
1/2 cup green onions, sliced
1/2 teaspoon salt

DIRECTIONS:
Place apricots in a small bowl of hot water and let sit for 10-15 minutes, then drain off the water. Now roughly chop the cauliflower and place it in a food processor and pulse to a rice consistency. In a large skillet, add 2 tablespoons of oil with garlic and onions and sauté until the onions are golden brown. This takes about 3-5 minutes. Then add the cauliflower and sauté for 8 minutes.
While the cauliflower is cooking, place the chickpeas and pistachios in a small pan and sauté with 1 teaspoon of oil and a pinch of salt until light and crisp. Once the cauliflower is golden brown, add in the chickpeas, spinach, apricots, and pistachios. Cook until the spinach turns bright green. Transfer to a serving platter and top with green onions.
Vegan Recipe

Cooking Time: 25 Minutes

Serving Size: 6-8

Cooking Appliance: Stove

Notes:

Sweet Potato Nachos

INGREDIENTS:
2 large sweet potatoes
guacamole (see page 153)
cooked pulled chicken
Megan's 5 minute beans
            (see page 151)
pico de gallo (see page 157)
corn (optional)
1 tablespoon avocado oil
1 teaspoon salt
1 teaspoon black pepper
1/2 teaspoon Lawry's Seasoned Salt

DIRECTIONS:
Preheat oven to 400° Fahrenheit.
Slice sweet potatoes into thin
circles and place on a baking sheet.
Drizzle oil, salt, pepper, and
Lawry's over the potatoes.
Toss the potatoes coating
them all in seasoning.
Place them in the oven for 30
minutes, flipping after 15 minutes.
To assemble, take sweet potatoes
and layer with guacamole, beans,
pico de gallo, corn, chicken, and
for an extra kick Frank's Red Hot
Sauce.

Cooking Time: 30 Minutes

Serving Size: 6

Cooking Appliance: Oven

Notes:

Pistachio Apricot Rice

INGREDIENTS:
1 box Lundberg organic whole
      grain rice & wild rice, garlic
      and basil, gluten free
1 cup Lundberg wild blend rice
whole grain, gluten free
1/2 cup Lundberg organic California
white jasmine rice, gluten free
1 can cooked lentils, rinsed
2/3 cup pistachios, chopped
2/3 cup apricots, chopped
low-sodium chicken broth
1 tsp Himalayan salt
1/2 teaspoon ground pepper

DIRECTIONS:
Make the box of Lundberg whole
grain rice & wild rice, garlic &
basil, gluten free according to
the box directions exactly. Follow
the directions on the back of the
package for each of the other two
Lundberg rice, but use the chicken
broth instead of water. Combine
all the cooked rice into one pot
and add the lentils, apricots, and
pistachios. Salt and pepper to taste.
Mix and enjoy!

Cooking Time: 30-35 Minutes

Serving Size: 8-10

Cooking Appliance: Stove

Notes:

pizzas

Peach Fig Pizza & Pesto Prosciutto Pizza

INGREDIENTS:

Peach Fig Pizza:
1 pizza crust or flatbread
1 peach, sliced
3 tablespoons melted fig jam
1/3 cup goat cheese, crumbled
3-4 slices prosciutto,
chopped
2-3 tablespoons Parmesan,
grated
balsamic glaze, to drizzle on top

Pesto Prosciutto Pizza:
1 pizza crust or flatbread
3 tablespoons pesto
(see page 97)
3-4 slices prosciutto,
chopped
1/3 cup feta, chopped
3 tablespoons Parmesan

DIRECTIONS:
Preheat oven to 400° Fahrenheit.
Layer all ingredients on top of the
crust or flatbread. Place in the
oven for 10-15 minutes until golden
brown.
Slice and enjoy!

Cooking Time: 15 Minutes

Serving Size: 4-6 each

Cooking Appliance: Stove

Notes:

White Pizza & Sausage Red Pepper Pizza

INGREDIENTS:

White Pizza:
1 pizza crust or flatbread
1/2 cup cooked Italian sausage
3 tablespoons olive oil
1/2 teaspoon Italian seasoning
1/3 cup feta cheese, crumbled
1 tablespoon fresh basil leaves, chopped
1/3 cup spinach, chopped
1/3-1/2 cup tomatoes, chopped

Sausage Red Pepper Pizza:
1 pizza crust or flatbread
3 tablespoons marinara sauce
1/2 cup cooked Italian sausage
1/3 cup feta cheese, crumbled
1 cup sautéd peppers
and onions
3 tablespoons Pecorino Romano, shredded
2 tablespoons fresh basil leaves, chopped

DIRECTIONS:
Preheat oven to 400° Fahrenheit. Layer all ingredients on top of the crust or flatbread. Place in the oven for 10-15 minutes until golden brown. Slice and enjoy!

Cooking Time: 15 Minutes

Serving Size: 4-6 each

Cooking Appliance: Oven

Notes:

pastas

Pesto Pasta & Sausage

INGREDIENTS:
3 cups rotini or pipe rigate
3 cups of broccoli, chopped
1 cup of grape tomatoes, quartered
2 cups of mushrooms, sliced (optional)
1/2 red onion, finely diced
1 tablespoon of minced garlic
2 large spicy chicken sausages
1/4 teaspoon of Italian seasoning
1/4 teaspoon of red pepper flakes
1/4 teaspoon of black pepper
1/4 teaspoon garlic salt
2 tablespoons of Parmesan
1/3 cup of pesto (see page 97)

DIRECTIONS:
Bring a large pot of water to a boil and lightly salt the water. Once the water has boiled add in your pasta and cook until done. In a medium skillet, crumble the chicken sausage into small pieces and cook until crispy. In a separate pan, add a dash of olive oil and combine with the garlic, onions, pepper, red pepper, garlic salt, and Italian seasoning. Cook on medium heat until the onions become translucent. Then add in mushrooms and chopped broccoli and cook until the broccoli is bright green and crispy. Finally add the chopped tomatoes and cooked sausage then heat until the tomatoes become soft and burst. Now in a large bowl, mix the pasta with the pesto and then add in your vegetable and sausage mixture. Top with Parmesan cheese and enjoy!

Cooking Time: 30-35 Minutes

Serving Size: 8-10

Cooking Appliance: Stove

Notes:

81

Mama Juju's Orzo Pasta Salad

INGREDIENTS:
1 small eggplant, diced
1 red bell pepper, diced
1 yellow bell pepper, diced
1 red onion, diced
2 garlic cloves, minced
1/3 cup olive oil
1 1/2 teaspoons kosher salt
1/2 teaspoon freshly ground black pepper
1/2 pound orzo
Dressing:
1/3 cup freshly squeezed lemon juice
1/3 cup good olive oil
1 teaspoon kosher salt
1/2 teaspoon freshly ground black pepper
To Assemble:
4 scallions, chopped (white and green parts)
1/4 cup pine nuts, toasted
3/4 pound good feta, 1/2" diced
15 fresh basil leaves, chopped

Cooking Time: 20-25 Minutes

Serving Size: 8-10

Cooking Appliance: Oven & Stove

Notes:

DIRECTIONS:
Preheat the oven to 425° Fahrenheit.
Toss the eggplant, bell peppers, onion, and garlic with the olive oil, salt, and pepper on a large baking sheet. Roast for 20-25 minutes, until browned, turning once with a spatula. Meanwhile, cook the orzo in boiling salted water for 7 to 9 minutes, until tender. Drain and transfer to a large serving bowl. Add the roasted vegetables to the pasta, scraping all of the liquid and seasonings from the roasting pan into the pasta bowl. For the dressing: Combine the lemon juice, olive oil, salt, and pepper and pour on the pasta and vegetables. Let cool to room temperature, then add the scallions, pignolis, feta, and basil. Adjust the seasonings, and serve at room temperature.

Green Pasta

INGREDIENTS:
1 jar pesto (see recipe page 97)
3 zucchinis
3 tablespoons pumpkin seeds
1 cup green peas
salt
black pepper
1 avocado
1/4 cup Pecorino Romano cheese, grated

DIRECTIONS:
Preheat the oven to 350° Fahrenheit.
First spiralize three zucchinis, and
set them aside in a bowl. In a small
skillet, toast your pumpkin seeds for 5
minutes with salt and pepper, stirring
occasionally to prevent burning.
Set those aside. Prepare your other
ingredients. Shave your cheese, dice the
avocado, and measure out the peas in
a large pan. Cook your zucchini noodles
for 2-3 minutes, until warm and place in
an oven-safe bowl. You do not want to
overcook the noodles! Add your zucchini
off heat and combine with pesto, peas,
and half your cheese. Add the chopped
avocado. Top your dish with remaining
cheese and toasted pumpkin seeds.
Place your dish in the oven for 3 minutes
to begin melting the cheese and enjoy!

Cooking Time: 5 Minutes

Serving Size: 6-8

Cooking Appliance: Oven & Stove

Notes:

Vegan Spaghetti Squash Noodles

INGREDIENTS:
1 spaghetti squash
1 tablespoon avocado oil
salt
black pepper
garlic salt

DIRECTIONS:
Preheat the oven to 425° Fahrenheit. First slice your spaghetti squash vertically in half and scoop out the seeds. Poke the outside of the squash with a fork. Then drizzle your oil over the two halves. Sprinkle with salt, pepper, and garlic salt. Roast for 15 minutes with the cut side up. Then flip your squash and roast for 20 minutes. Once you take the squash out of the oven, use two forks to shred the squash into noodles and place in a bowl. Top with salt, pepper, and your favorite sauce!

Cooking Time: 35 Minutes

Serving Size: 6-8

Cooking Appliance: Oven

Notes:

sauces

Eggs In Purgatory

INGREDIENTS:
1 red bell pepper
1/2 onion
1 clove garlic, minced
6 fresh basil leaves, chopped
1 tablespoon of olive oil
1/4 teaspoon black pepper
1/2 teaspoon salt
1/2 teaspoon oregano
1/2 teaspoon garlic salt
1/2 teaspoon red chili flakes
1/2 - 28 oz can of whole peeled tomatoes
2 eggs
2 tablespoons Pecorino Romano cheese, grated

Cooking Time: 10 Minutes

Serving Size: 8-10

Cooking Appliance: Stove

Notes:

DIRECTIONS:
First prepare your veggies!
Thinly slice your onion and slice your pepper into long strips. Add olive oil to a pan and place on medium heat. Add all your chopped veggies, garlic, and basil to a pan. Cook until the onions have browned and the peppers begin to soften. Purée the tomatoes in a food processor, then add to the pan with the black pepper, salt, garlic salt, oregano, and red chili flakes. Let this simmer for 5-10 minutes until it begins to bubble.Then add your 2 eggs on opposite side of the pan and cover the eggs with sauce leaving the yolk exposed. Add your cheese over the eggs and sauce. Let this cook for at least 5 minutes. It is ready to eat when the eggs are cooked to your liking. This is best served with a warm piece of toast on the side that is sprinkled with Italian seasoning!

Bolognese

INGREDIENTS:
1/4 cup olive oil
1 medium onion, minced
2 garlic cloves, minced
1 pound Italian sausage
2 - 28 oz cans of crushed tomatoes
1 1/2 teaspoon dried oregano
1 bunch fresh basil leaves, chopped
1/2 teaspoon Lawry's Seasoned Salt
1/2 teaspoon salt
1/2 teaspoon black pepper
1/2 cup Pecorino Romano cheese,
        grated
1/4 teaspoon crushed red chili flakes

DIRECTIONS:
In a large skillet, heat the oil over medium heat for 5 minutes. Then add in the onion and garlic and sauté until the onion is tender, about 8 minutes. Increase the heat to high and add in the sausage. Sauté until the meat is cooked and begins to brown. (This is important for flavor development.) Add the remaining ingredients except the cheese and cook on medium to low heat for 30 minutes. Then stir in the cheese, cook another 10 minutes and add more salt and pepper to taste. Serve alone or with pasta and enjoy!

Cooking Time: 55-60 Minutes

Serving Size: 8-10

Cooking Appliance: Stove

Notes:

Marinara

INGREDIENTS:
1/3 cup olive oil
2 small onions, chopped
2 garlic cloves, minced
3/4 teaspoon salt
1/2 teaspoon black pepper
1 - 28 oz can crushed tomatoes
1 - 28 oz can whole tomatoes
(crush them with a hand mixer)
1/4 cup fresh basil leaves, chopped
1/2 cup Pecorino Romano cheese,
grated

DIRECTIONS:
In a large pot, heat oil over
medium-high heat for 3-5 minutes.
Then add the onions and garlic and
sauté. Cook for around 10 minutes
until the onions are softened. Add
in the salt, pepper, and basil. Then
add the tomatoes and cook for
30 minutes on medium-low heat.
Stir in the cheese, cook another 10
minutes, and add more salt and
pepper to taste. Turn off the heat
and enjoy!

Cooking Time: 50-55 Minutes

Serving Size: 6-8

Cooking Appliance: Stove

Notes:

Pesto

INGREDIENTS:
3 cups fresh basil leaves
1 cup olive oil
1/2 teaspoon salt
1/2 teaspoon black pepper
1-2 garlic cloves
1/4 cup pine nuts
2 tablespoons Pecorino
Romano cheese, grated
2 tablespoons Parmesan
cheese, grated

DIRECTIONS:
Add all the ingredients into a food
processor and blend on high until
desired consistency is reached.

Cooking Time: 10 Minutes

Serving Size: 8-10

Cooking Appliance:

Notes:

Nut-Free Pesto

INGREDIENTS:
2 cups fresh basil leaves
1 garlic clove
1 cup spinach
2 tablespoons lemon juice
1 tablespoon olive oil
1 tablespoon chicken broth
1 teaspoon salt
1 teaspoon pepper
2 tablespoons Parmesan, grated

DIRECTIONS:
Add all the ingredients
to a food processor and blend until
smooth. If the mixture is too thick,
add more lemon juice or oil
depending on the acidity of the
pesto.

Cooking Time: 10-15 Minutes

Serving Size: 4

Cooking Appliance:

Notes:

salads

Watermelon Mint Salad

INGREDIENTS:
1 small watermelon, cut 1" chunks
1/4 cup olive oil
1/4 cup red onion, diced
2 tablespoons lime juice
1/2 teaspoon salt
1/4 teaspoon black pepper
1/4 cup mint, chopped
4 oz sheep milk feta, crumbled

DIRECTIONS:
In a small bowl whisk together the oil, lime juice, salt, and pepper. Pour the dressing over the chilled diced watermelon along with the mint and onion. Toss gently to combine and sprinkle with crumbled feta and serve immediately.

Cooking Time: 10 Minutes

Serving Size: 6-8

Cooking Appliance: Stove

Notes:

Beet & Goat Cheese Salad

INGREDIENTS:
3 red beets
1/3 cup goat cheese
1 cup chopped
micro greens
1/2 orange
1 lemon
1 teaspoon stone-ground mustard
1/2 teaspoon salt
1/4 teaspoon pepper
1 teaspoon olive oil

DIRECTIONS:
First prepare your beets.
You can either do this in the
microwave or by boiling. Microwave:
Peel beets and cut into quarters,
adding 1/4 cup of water to the bowl,
and microwave for 5-7 minutes
checking occasionally with a fork.
Boiling: Peel your beets and place
them whole in a pot of water and boil
for 45 minutes, until tender.
In a small bowl, juice orange and
lemon. Add in the salt, pepper, oil, and
mustard. Mix to combine. Dice the
beets, and add them to a bowl with
the goat cheese, micro greens, and
dressing. Mix the salad until the goat
cheese is well incorporated. Serve
with a pinch of flaky salt on top and
enjoy!

Cooking Time: 5-7 Minutes

Serving Size: 4-6

Cooking Appliance: Microwave or Stove

Notes:

Three Bean Salad

INGREDIENTS:
1 large red pepper, diced
1 large yellow pepper, diced
1 large orange pepper, diced
1 medium red onion, diced
1 can black beans, drained
1 can black-eyed peas, drained
1 can pinto beans, drained
1 small package frozen yellow corn,
    thawed

DRESSING:
3 1/2 tablespoons coconut sugar
3/4 cup apple cider vinegar
1/2 cup avocado oil
1 teaspoon water
2 teaspoons salt
1 teaspoon pepper

DIRECTIONS:
First rinse the beans and dice the onion and peppers. In a large bowl, combine all the vegetables and beans. In a sauce pan, heat the dressing and bring to a boil. Remove from heat and let cool then pour over the bean mixture and toss to combine.

Vegan Recipe

Recipe inspired by Aunt Sherry.

Cooking Time: 10 Minutes

Serving Size: 8-10

Cooking Appliance: Stove

Notes:

Modern
Tuna Salad

INGREDIENTS:
1/2 cucumber
1 can tuna
2 tablespoons fresh basil, chopped
1 tablespoon fresh cilantro, chopped
2 tablespoons red onions, chopped
1 tablespoon lemon juice
1 tablespoon red wine vinegar
1/2 tablespoon apple cider vinegar
1/2 tablespoon olive oil
1/4 teaspoon salt
1/2 teaspoon pepper
1/4 teaspoon Lawry's Seasoned Salt
pinch of red chili flakes

DIRECTIONS:
First chop the cucumber into
1/2 inch pieces, drain the can of tuna,
and add them to a bowl.
Then add the remaining ingredients
and mix well to combine. Serve
alone or with chips
as an appetizer!

Cooking Time: 10 Minutes

Serving Size: 2

Cooking Appliance:

Notes:

Cucumber
Salad

INGREDIENTS:
1 large cucumber
1/4 teaspoon sea salt
1/4 teaspoon pepper
1/4 teaspoon Lawry's Seasoned Salt
3 tablespoons apple
cider vinegar
1 teaspoon red wine vinegar

DIRECTIONS:
First peel the cucumber, then slice
it and place in a bowl. Then add
the remaining ingredients and mix
well. Let soak for at least 10 minutes
before serving. Enjoy!

Vegan Recipe

Cooking Time: 10 Minutes

Serving Size: 4

Cooking Appliance:

Notes:

Ramen Noodle Salad

INGREDIENTS:
16 oz bag coleslaw
1 cup slivered almonds
2 packages ramen noodles,
chicken flavor

DRESSING:
1 cup avocado oil
6 tablespoons apple cider vinegar
6 tablespoons sugar
2 packets soup flavoring from the
ramen
salt and pepper to taste

DIRECTIONS:
First heat your oven to 300°
Fahrenheit. Crush the ramen
noodle packets with a rolling pin
and add them to a sheet tray with
the silvered almonds. Put the
tray into the oven and bake for
20 minutes. Stir after 10 minutes.
Mix the dressing and add it to the
salad. Wait to add the almonds and
toasted noodles until you are ready
to serve.

Cooking Time: 20 Minutes

Serving Size: 8-10

Cooking Appliance: Oven

Notes:

Kale
Apple Salad

INGREDIENTS:
1/4 cup roasted sunflower seeds
1/2 cup olive oil
1/2 teaspoon salt
1/2 teaspoon ground black pepper
1/2 small shallot, chopped
1/4 cup fresh lemon juice
1 small garlic clove, minced
1 teaspoon dijon mustard
1 large bunch tuscan kale (spines removed)
6 oz Brussels sprouts
2 oz Parmesan cheese, shredded
1 pink lady apple

DIRECTIONS:
Make the vinaigrette. In a small bowl, mix together olive oil, chopped shallot, lemon juice, minced garlic clove, and dijon mustard, and season with salt and pepper. Thinly slice the kale and Brussel sprouts and transfer to a large bowl. Grate Parmesan into a separate bowl. Finely chop one apple and set it aside. Add the dressing to the kale mixture and toss thoroughly with your hands to soften the kale. Add the cheese, apples, and sunflower seeds to the bowl and toss lightly. Now serve and enjoy!

Cooking Time: 10 Minutes

Serving Size: 6-8

Cooking Appliance:

Notes:

Mama's Italian Salad

INGREDIENTS:
2 romaine heads, chopped
2 cups fresh baby spinach
1/2 cup grape tomatoes, quartered
1/4 cup English cucumber, quartered
1/4 cup red onion, diced
1/4 cup yellow pepper, diced
1/4 cup feta cheese, diced
1/4 cup Pecorino Romano cheese
1/2 honey crisp apple, diced
3/4 teaspoon Lawry's Seasoned Salt
1/2 teaspoon ground pepper
1 teaspoon ground salt
1 teaspoon Italian seasoning
1/3 cup olive oil
1 1/2 tablespoons red wine vinegar
2 teaspoons lemon juice

DIRECTIONS:
Clean and chop the romaine, spinach, red onion, cucumber, yellow pepper, and grape tomatoes. Place in a bowl. Mix together in a separate bowl all the spices, olive oil, lemon, and vinegar. Add the dressing to the vegetables, feta, Pecorino Romano, and toss. And lastly place the apples on top. Enjoy!

Cooking Time: 10 Minutes

Serving Size: 6-8

Cooking Appliance:

Notes:

Simple Arugula Salad

INGREDIENTS:
3 cups arugula
2 cups spinach
1/2 cup fresh squeezed lemon juice
1/2 cup olive oil
1/2 teaspoon salt
1/4 teaspoon black pepper
1/4 cup Parmesan cheese, shredded
1/3 cup goat cheese, crumbled
1/4 cup pumpkin seeds, roasted

DIRECTIONS:
In a small bowl, mix to combine the lemon, oil, black pepper, and salt.
Add the greens to a bowl with the cheese and pour the dressing over the salad and mix.
Sprinkle pumpkin seeds on top.
Serve immediately and enjoy!

Cooking Time: 10 Minutes

Serving Size: 6-8

Cooking Appliance:

Notes:

Egg-Free Caesar Salad

INGREDIENTS:
3 heads Romaine, chopped
1 clove garlic, chopped
2 tablespoons lemon juice
1 teaspoon Worcestershire sauce
1 teaspoon whole grain mustard
1/2 cup Parmesan or Pecorino
Romano cheese, shredded
1/3 cup olive oil
1/2 teaspoon pepper
3/4 teaspoon salt

DIRECTIONS:

SALAD DIRECTIONS:
Place garlic, lemon, Worcestershire, mustard, olive oil, pepper and salt into a small bowl and mix. Place cleaned and chopped Romaine into a larger bowl. Toss the oil mixture, cheese, and Romaine all together. Then top with the croutons and more cheese.

CROUTONS:
Place 2 tablespoons oil and 1 teaspoon Italian seasoning in a frying pan and toss. Then add 1 1/2 cups chopped baguette bread and continue to toss and cook for 5-7 minutes until desired crispiness!

Cooking Time: 10 Minutes

Serving Size: 6-8

Cooking Appliance: Stove

Notes:

121

Quinoa Kale Salad

INGREDIENTS:
1/2 cup uncooked quinoa or
3/4 cup cooked quinoa
6 cups kale, chopped
1 cup apples, chopped,
or pomegranate seeds
1/4 cup dried cranberries
1/3 cup feta, crumbled
1/4 cup Parmesan, shredded
1/3 cup macadiamia nuts or
pine nuts, chopped

DRESSING:
1/2 cup olive oil
2 tablespoons apple cider vinegar
1/2 teaspoon dijon mustard
1 1/2 teaspoons honey
1/2 teaspoon salt
1/2 teaspoon pepper

DIRECTIONS:
First cook the quinoa, following the
directions on the package.
In a large bowl, mix together the kale,
quinoa, fruit, dried cranberries, and
nuts. Make the dressing, whisk
together olive oil, apple cider
vinegar, dijon mustard, honey,
salt, and pepper. Pour the dressing
over the salad and massage with your
hands to soften the kale. Then stir in
the feta and Parmesan, and enjoy!

Cooking Time: 20 Minutes

Serving Size: 6-8

Cooking Appliance:

Notes:

123

Strawberry Salad

INGREDIENTS:

SALAD INGREDIENTS:
8 oz baby spinach
1 cup strawberries,
sliced
1/3 cup pecans,
chopped and toasted
1/4 cup goat cheese

DRESSING:
1/4 cup balsamic vinegar
1/4 teaspoon stone-ground mustard
1 tablespoon raw honey
1/4 cup olive oil
1/4 teaspoon salt
1/4 teaspoon pepper

DIRECTIONS:
Prepare the spinach.
Add the vinegar, honey, salt, pepper, mustard, and oil to a bowl. Mix to combine then pour over the salad.
To toast the pecans add them to a skillet and roast on medium heat for 5 minutes. Toss with the strawberries, toasted pecans and goat cheese, and enjoy!

Cooking Time: 10 Minutes

Serving Size: 6-8

Cooking Appliance: Stove

Notes:

Greek
Salad

INGREDIENTS:
2 cups grape tomatoes, cut in quarters
3 Romaine heads, chopped
2 cups cucumber, cut in quarters
1/2 cup red onion, diced
2/3 cup feta cheese, diced
1/2 teaspoon Lawry's Seasoned Salt
1/2 teaspoon ground pepper
3/4 teaspoon ground sea salt
1 teaspoon of Greek seasoning
1/3 cup olive oil
2 tablespoons red wine vinegar

DIRECTIONS:
Clean and chop the romaine, red onions, cucumbers, and grape tomatoes. Place in a bowl.
Mix together in a separate bowl all the spices, olive oil and vinegar. Add the dressing and feta to the vegetables, and toss. Enjoy!

Cooking Time: 10 Minutes

Serving Size: 6-8

Cooking Appliance:

Notes:

Brussels Sprout Salad

INGREDIENTS:
5 cups thinly sliced Brussels sprouts
2/3 cup Parmesan cheese, shaved
1/3 cup slivered almonds, toasted
1/4 cup olive oil
1/2 teaspoon salt
1/2 teaspoon pepper
3 tablespoons lemon juice
1/3 cup feta cheese, crumbled
1/4 cup red onion

DIRECTIONS:
Add the oil, salt, pepper, and lemon juice to a bowl and mix. In a large bowl, add in the Brussels sprouts, Parmesan cheese, feta cheese, red onions, and almonds, then mix to combine. Pour in the dressing, mix thoroughly, and enjoy!

Cooking Time: 20 Minutes

Serving Size: 6-8

Cooking Appliance:

Notes:

meat dishes

Fig Turkey Burgers

INGREDIENTS:
1 tablespoon avocado oil
1 package ground turkey
1/4 cup onion
1 tablespoon fig jam
1 bunch broccolini, chopped
1/2 teaspoon black pepper
1/4 cup goat cheese, crumbled
1/2 teaspoon salt
1/4 teaspoon garlic salt
1 pack of arugula
2 packs of Pretzilla Slider Buns

DIRECTIONS:
Dice the onion and place in a large bowl and mix with the ground turkey. Form the mixture into 6-8 small burgers and season both sides with salt and pepper. Add them to a large pan and cook until the internal temperature reads 165° Fahrenheit, flipping halfway through. In a separate pan, sauté the broccolini with salt, garlic salt, pepper, and avocado oil. Cook until the broccolini has turned bright green and add to the plate. Place the turkey burger on a pretzel bun slider or enjoy alone. Top with fig jam, arugula, and crumbled goat cheese. Enjoy!

Cooking Time: 20-25 Minutes

Serving Size: 6-8

Cooking Appliance: Stove

Notes:

133

Feta Burgers

INGREDIENTS:
1 pound ground beef
1/3 cup feta, crumbled
1/4 cup Worcestershire sauce
1/2 tablespoon Canadian steak
      seasoning
2 packs of Pretzilla Slider Buns
Chipotle Mayo (see page 167)

DIRECTIONS:
Place all the ingredients into a
bowl. Mix together and then form
into 6-8 patties. Place patties on
a sheet pan and sprinkle both
sides with additional Canadian
steak seasoning. Cook on grill
or in a frying pan to an internal
temperature of 165° Fahrenheit.
Toast the Pretzel Buns on the grill
until golden brown. Finally spread
the Chipotle Mayo on the buns,
and add the burger and your
favorite toppings. Enjoy!

Cooking Time: 10 Minutes

Serving Size: 6-8

Cooking Appliance: Grill or Stove

Notes:

Herb Turkey Burgers

INGREDIENTS:
1 package ground turkey
2 tablespoons red onion, chopped
2 tablespoons cilantro, chopped
1 teaspoon chives, chopped
1 clove garlic, minced
1 tablespoon fresh basil leaves, chopped
1/2 teaspoon salt
1/4 teaspoon black pepper
1/4 teaspoon garlic salt
1/4 teaspoon Italian seasoning
Basil Guacamole (see page 155)
Sliced Tomato
1 head of crunchy lettuce
2 packs of Pretzilla Sliders Buns

DIRECTIONS:
In a large bowl, combine all the ingredients and stir until mixture is combined. Form into 6-8 patties. In a large skillet, add in the patties and cook until the meat reaches 165° Fahrenheit. Place the burger on a pretzel bread slider or enjoy alone. Top with the basil guacamole, tomato, lettuce, and enjoy!

Cooking Time: 15 Minutes

Serving Size: 6-8

Cooking Appliance: Stove

Notes:

Dad's Grilled Teriyaki Salmon

INGREDIENTS:
10 oz Soy Vay Teriyaki Marinade & Sauce
2 pounds boneless, skinless salmon filets
1 tablespoon (Chef Paul Prudhomme Magic Seasoning Blends® Blackened Redfish Magic)

DIRECTIONS:
Add all the ingredients to a plastic bag and marinade for 4 hours. Remove from the bag and add to a grill mat. Cook on the grill for 2-2.5 minutes per side at medium-high heat. Then enjoy!

Cooking Time: 4-5 Minutes

Serving Size: 6-8

Cooking Appliance: Grill

Notes:

Italian Meatballs

INGREDIENTS:
1 lb lean ground beef
2 eggs
½ cup cold water
1 cup Italian-style bread crumbs
1 cup Pecorino Romano cheese, grated
1 tablespoon dried parsley
1 tablespoon olive oil
1 garlic clove, chopped
3 tablespoons fresh basil, chopped
1 ½ teaspoons kosher salt
1 tsp Italian seasoning
½ teaspoon Lawry's seasoned salt
¼ teaspoon pepper

DIRECTIONS:
Preheat the oven to 350° Fahrenheit. Sauté olive oil and chopped garlic until golden and then pour into a larger mixing bowl. In another smaller bowl, mix together the eggs and water. Add beef, breadcrumbs, chopped basil, and all the dried seasonings to the larger mixing bowl and mix well. You will probably need to use your hands. Then add the egg mixture to the meat mixture and mix some more! Form into 1-inch balls and place on a nonstick baking pan. Bake for 20 minutes, flipping the meatballs halfway through. Remove from the oven and enjoy!

Cooking Time: 20 Minutes

Serving Size: 8-10

Cooking Appliance: Stove & Oven

Notes:

Cauliflower Chicken Fried Rice

INGREDIENTS:
1 packet riced cauliflower
(frozen or microwaveable pouch)
1/4 onion, diced
1/2 cup cooked pulled chicken
3 tablespoons green peas
1 tablespoon rice vinegar
2 tablespoons liquid coconut aminos
1/4 cup chicken broth
1/4 teaspoon red chili flakes
1/4 teaspoon black pepper
1/2 teaspoon salt
1 garlic clove, minced
1-inch piece ginger, minced

DIRECTIONS:
First drain your riced cauliflower and set aside. Then in a bowl, combine the coconut aminos, rice vinegar, chili flakes, salt, pepper, garlic, chicken broth, and ginger. Add your cauliflower and the sauce mixture to a large pan with your diced onion and green peas. Cook until the garlic begins to bubble (around 3-5 minutes). Then add pulled cooked chicken and heat for 3 minutes. Serve and enjoy!

Cooking Time: 6-8 Minutes

Serving Size: 4

Cooking Appliance: Stove

Notes:

dips & sides

Tonia's Hummus

INGREDIENTS:
2 cans chickpeas, drained
3 cloves garlic, chopped
1/4 cup tahini
1/4 cup fresh lemon juice
2 teaspoons sea salt
1 1/2 cups extra virgin olive oil

DIRECTIONS:
Chop garlic in food processor.
Add the drained chickpeas and
blend until finely ground. Then add
tahini, salt, lemon, and olive oil. Add
the olive oil slowly and blend until
smooth.

Vegan Recipe

Cooking Time: 5 Minutes

Serving Size: 8-10

Cooking Appliance: Blender

Notes:

Beet Hummus

INGREDIENTS:
2 medium or 1 large beet, peeled
1 - 15 oz can chickpeas, drained
1 teaspoon salt
1 lemon zest and juice
1 teaspoon black pepper
1/4 cup tahini
1 tablespoon olive oil
1 garlic clove

DIRECTIONS:
First prepare your beets.
You can either do this in the microwave or by boiling. Microwave: Peel beets and cut into quarters, adding 1/4 cup of water to the bowl, and microwave for 5-7 minutes checking occasionally with a fork. Boiling: Place whole peeled beets in a pot of water and boil for 45 minutes, until tender. Meantime, zest your lemon, then squeeze the juice into a bowl. Once the beets are cooked, add them to a food processor with one can of drained chickpeas and pulse to combine. Then add your salt, oil, lemon juice, tahini, lemon zest, and pepper to the food processor. Mix on high until desired consistency is reached. Wait until cooled or enjoy right away! Store in the refrigerator in an airtight container.
Vegan Recipe

Cooking Time: 45 Minutes

Serving Size: 8-10

Cooking Appliance: Microwave & Stove

Notes:

Megan's
5-Minute Beans

INGREDIENTS:
1 can black beans
2 tablespoons butter
Lawry's Seasoned Salt to taste

DIRECTIONS:
Drain the beans in a strainer and
rinse with water. Add butter to pan.
Then add beans and Lawry's.
Cook on medium heat for 5
minutes, stirring consistently until
done.

Cooking Time: 5 Minutes

Serving Size: 6-8

Cooking Appliance: Stove

Notes:

Guacamole

INGREDIENTS:
1 avocado
1/4 teaspoon salt
1/4 teaspoon black pepper
1/4 teaspoon Lawry's Seasoned Salt
1 lime, juiced
2 tablespoons cilantro, chopped
2 tablespoons onion, diced
5 cherry tomatoes, diced

DIRECTIONS:
Add the avocado to a bowl but do not mash. Prepare the rest of your ingredients and add them into the bowl. Now mash to your desired consistency and enjoy!

Vegan Recipe

Cooking Time: 5 Minutes

Serving Size: 2-4

Cooking Appliance:

Notes:

Basil Guacamole

INGREDIENTS:
1 avocado
1/2 cup basil leaves
1/4 cup cilantro
1 garlic clove
1/2 teaspoon salt
1 teaspoon pepper
1/2 teaspoon Lawry's Seasoned Salt
1 lime, juiced
1/8 red onion

DIRECTIONS:
Add all the ingredients to a blender
and mix until combined. Serve
and enjoy as a dip, spread for toast,
topping for a burger, or anything
you want!

Vegan Recipe

Cooking Time: 5 Minutes

Serving Size: 2-4

Cooking Appliance: Blender

Notes:

Pico De Gallo

INGREDIENTS:
1 lime, juiced
1/4 cup cilantro, finely chopped
1 jalapeño, diced
1/3 cup red onion, chopped
2 heirloom
tomatoes, diced
1/2 teaspoon salt
1/4 teaspoon
black pepper

DIRECTIONS:
Prepare all the vegetables and add
them to a bowl. Juice one lime into
the bowl and add the seasoning.
Serve immediately and enjoy!

Vegan Recipe

Cooking Time: 5 Minutes

Serving Size: 4

Cooking Appliance:

Notes:

Roasted Corn Salsa

INGREDIENTS:
1 can corn, drained
1/2 onion, diced
1/4 cup cilantro, chopped
1 tablespoon olive oil
1 teaspoon paprika
1/2 lime
1/2 teaspoon chili powder
1/4 teaspoon salt
1/4 teaspoon black pepper

DIRECTIONS:
Add the corn, onion, and spices to a pan with 1 tablespoon of oil. Cook on medium heat for 7-10 minutes until the corn and onions begin to brown. Remove from heat, add in the cilantro and a squeeze of fresh lime juice then enjoy!

Vegan Recipe

Cooking Time: 7-10 Minutes

Serving Size: 6-8

Cooking Appliance: Stove

Notes:

Avocado
Corn Salsa

INGREDIENTS:
1 can corn, drained
1 avocado, chopped
1/2 cup tomatoes, chopped
1 lime, juiced
2 tablespoons cilantro, chopped
1/2 teaspoon Lawry's Seasoned Salt
1/2 teaspoon black pepper
1/2 teaspoon salt

DIRECTIONS:
Add all the ingredients to a bowl,
mix thoroughly, with the lime juice
and spices. Enjoy!

Vegan Recipe

Cooking Time: 5 Minutes

Serving Size: 6-8

Cooking Appliance:

Notes:

Simple
Salsa Verde

INGREDIENTS:
2 large green heirloom tomatoes
    or tomatillos
1/2 cup fresh cilantro
1/3 cup lime juice
1 white onion
2 teaspoons salt
1 teaspoon black pepper
2 jalapeños, seeded

DIRECTIONS:
In a large pot of water, boil the green tomatoes or tomatillos and jalapeño for 15 minutes.
Add the remaining ingredients to a blender and mix to combine.
Once the vegetables are done, drain off the water then add them to the blender and mix to your desired consistency. Pour into Mason jars and place in the refrigerator to cool and enjoy!

Vegan Recipe

Cooking Time: 15 Minutes

Serving Size: 10

Cooking Appliance: Blender & Stove

Notes:

Salsa Roja

INGREDIENTS:
6 drieds guajillo chiles
3 dried ancho chiles
3 Roma tomatoes
1/2 onion
3 garlic cloves
1/2 teaspoon Mexican oregano
1 teaspoon salt
1/2 teaspoon black pepper
1 teaspoon apple cider vinegar
2 1/2 cups water
1 tablespoon olive oil
1/4 cup fresh cilantro

DIRECTIONS:
Preheat the oven to 400° Fahrenheit.
First remove the seeds from the dried
chiles and chop into large pieces. Roast
the tomatoes in the oven for 15 minutes.
Chop the onion and mash the garlic
cloves. In a large pan, add the oil, onion,
garlic, oregano, salt, and pepper.
Cook for 10-15 minutes then add in the
dried chiles, and cook for 5 minutes until
the chiles have softened. Then add in
the roasted tomatoes and water, and
let cook for another 15 minutes. Add the
mixture to a blender with cilantro and
cider vinegar. Blend until the desired
consistency is reached. Add salt and
pepper to taste. Add to Mason jars, store
in the refrigerator, let cool, and enjoy!
Vegan Recipe

Cooking Time: 25-30 Minutes

Serving Size: 10

Cooking Appliance: Blender, Oven, & Stove

Notes:

Chipotle Mayo

INGREDIENTS:
2 tablespoons avocado mayonnaise
1 tablespoon Frank's Red Hot Sauce
1 teaspoon pickled jalapeños, chopped

DIRECTIONS:
Add all the ingredients to a bowl and whisk to combine. Enjoy with sweet potato fries, burgers, sandwiches, burritos, and so much more!

Cooking Time: 5 Minutes

Serving Size: 2

Cooking Appliance:

Notes:

Pickled Onions

INGREDIENTS:
1 cup water for brine
1/2 cup white or apple cider vinegar
1 teaspoon salt
2 tablespoons coconut sugar
8 whole black peppercorns
1 medium red onion, thinly sliced
3 cups water to boil

DIRECTIONS:
Start by adding 2 cups of water to a pot to boil for later. Now let's make the brine! Add your water, vinegar, salt, sugar, and peppercorns to a bowl. Mix until the sugar is dissolved. Add the onion slices to a bowl and pour the boiling water over them. Let the onions steep for 2 minutes, then drain the water from the bowl. Add your onions to a Mason jar and pour in your brine, covering all the onions. Screw the lid onto the jar and let the onions sit in your refrigerator for a least 5 hours before enjoying. They only get better with time. Congratulations! You know how to make fermented foods now! That wasn't too hard!

Vegan Recipe

Cooking Time: 7-10 Minutes

Serving Size: 10

Cooking Appliance: Stove

Notes:

desserts

Peanut Butter Banana Chocolate Cookies

INGREDIENTS:
1 cup organic quick-cooking oats
1 mashed ripe banana
1/4 cup chocolate chips
5 tablespoons powdered
peanut butter
1 tablespoon peanut butter
1/3 cup almond flour
1/2 teaspoon cinnamon
2 tablespoons water
1/4 cup egg whites
3 tablespoons almond milk
1 teaspoon baking powder

DIRECTIONS:
Preheat oven to 350° Fahrenheit.
Add mashed banana to a
bowl with oats, flour, egg whites,
milk, powdered peanut butter,
cinnamon, water, baking powder,
and chocolate chips and mix to
combine. Scoop the dough into
tablespoon-sized balls and place
on a baking sheet. Bake for 12-15
minutes until the bottoms are
golden brown. Cool and enjoy!

Cooking Time: 12-15 Minutes

Serving Size: 20

Cooking Appliance: Oven

Notes:

Fluffy Pumpkin Cookies

INGREDIENTS:
1/2 cup + 2 tablespoons almond flour
1/2 tablespoon coconut flour
1/3 cup golden monk fruit
        sweetener
4 tablespoons pumpkin puree
2 teaspoons pumpkin spice
2 1/4 tablespoons vegan butter
1/2 teaspoon vanilla extract
3/4 teaspoon baking powder
1 egg
1/4 teaspoon salt

DIRECTIONS:
Preheat oven to 325° Fahrenheit. Beat the egg with monk fruit sweetener, pumpkin puree, and cold butter. Add the remaining ingredients to the mixture and stir together. Scoop into tablespoon-sized balls and place on a baking sheet. Bake for 15-20 minutes until the bottoms are golden brown. Serve and enjoy!

Cooking Time: 15-20 Minutes

Serving Size: 15

Cooking Appliance: Oven

Notes:

Oatmeal Fruit Cookies

INGREDIENTS:
2 ripe bananas
1/4 cup avocado oil
2 tablespoons coconut sugar
1 egg
1 teaspoon vanilla
1 teaspoon baking powder
1 pinch sea salt
1/2 cup almond flour
1 cup rolled oats
1/3 cup raisins or dried figs or cranberries

DIRECTIONS:
Preheat oven to 350° Fahrenheit. Mash bananas in a bowl. Mix in the oil, sugar, egg, vanilla, salt, and baking powder. Add in the flour, oats, and dried fruit and combine. Bake for 15-18 minutes until the bottoms are golden brown. Serve and enjoy!

Cooking Time: 15-18 Minutes

Serving Size: 15

Cooking Appliance: Oven

Notes:

Lemon Cookies

INGREDIENTS:
2 cups almond flour
1/2 teaspoon baking powder
1/2 teaspoon salt
1/2 cup coconut sugar
1 1/2 tablespoons lemon zest
1/3 cup lemon juice
1/3 cup coconut oil
1 large egg
1 teaspoon vanilla
1 teaspoon fresh lemon zest

DIRECTIONS:
Preheat oven to 350° Fahrenheit. In a large bowl, combine all the ingredients and mix. Scoop into tablespoon-size balls. Cook for 11-13 minutes until bottoms are golden brown. Serve and enjoy!

Cooking Time: 11-13 Minutes

Serving Size: 15

Cooking Appliance: Oven

Notes:

Chocolate
Power Cookies

INGREDIENTS:
2 medium bananas
1/2 cup ground flax
1 cup organic quick-cooking oats
1/4 cup slivered almonds
1/4 cup mini
chocolate chips
1/4 cup shredded unsweetened
coconut
1/4 cup egg whites
1/2 teaspoon
baking powder
1 teaspoon vanilla
1/4 teaspoon salt
1 teaspoon cinnamon
1 tablespoon chia seeds
1 tablespoon cocoa powder
2 tablespoons nut milk

DIRECTIONS:
Preheat oven to 350° Fahrenheit.
Mash two ripe bananas in a bowl.
Add in remaining ingredients
and mix to combine. Scoop into
25 small balls. Place on a baking
sheet. Bake for 15 minutes until the
bottoms of the cookies are golden
brown.

Cooking Time: 15 Minutes

Serving Size: 25

Cooking Appliance: Oven

Notes:

Carrot
Breakfast Cookies

INGREDIENTS:
1 cup quick-cooking oats
1 cup almond flour
1 cup carrots, grated
2 teaspoons cinnamon
1 teaspoon baking powder
1/2 cup maple syrup
1/3 cup coconut oil
1/4 cup egg whites

ICING:
2 tablespoons coconut
butter, softened
3 tablespoons maple syrup
1/2 teaspoon cinnamon

DIRECTIONS:
Preheat oven to 350° Fahrenheit.
Combine dry ingredients in a bowl
and then add in wet ingredients.
Mix together and place on baking
sheet in one inch balls. Bake for 10-
15 minutes. Let cookies cool. Then
mix together icing ingredients and
drizzle on top of cookies.

Cooking Time: 10-15 Minutes

Serving Size: 25

Cooking Appliance: Oven

Notes:

Loft House
Sugar Cookie

INGREDIENTS:
1/2 cup unsalted butter, softened
3/4 cup granulated sugar
1 large egg
1/3 cup plain Greek yogurt
1 teaspoon vanilla
1/4 teaspoon almond extract
1 1/2 cups almond flour
1/4 cup tapioca flour
1 1/2 tablespoons cornstarch
1/2 teaspoon baking powder
1/2 teaspoon baking soda
1/4 teaspoon cream of tartar (optional)
1/3 teaspoon salt

FROSTING INGREDIENTS:
1 teaspoon vanilla
2 1/2 cups powdered sugar
3 tablespoons unsalted butter
rainbow sprinkles

Cooking Time: 11-13 Minutes

Serving Size: 25

Cooking Appliance: Oven

Notes:

DIRECTIONS:
Preheat oven to 375° Fahrenheit. Beat butter and sugar on medium speed until fluffy, then add in the egg and beat until incorporated. Then add in the vanilla and yogurt and beat on low speed until combined.In a separate bowl, combine dry ingredients then mix them into the wet ingredients. Cover the bowl and refrigerate for one hour. Form into tablespoon-sized balls and place on a parchment-lined baking sheet. Bake for 11-13 minutes until light golden brown on top.

FROSTING DIRECTIONS:
Beat the butter with the powdered sugar, food coloring, and vanilla. Ice cookies and top with sprinkles!

185

Blueberry Loaf Cake

INGREDIENTS:
1/2 cup vegan butter, room temp.
1/2 cup coconut oil, room temp.
2 cups almond flour
1/2 cup tapioca flour
1 teaspoon cinnamon
1/2 teaspoon baking soda
1/2 teaspoon salt
1 1/2 cups coconut sugar or
golden monk fruit sweetener
3 eggs
1 tablespoon lemon zest
1 cup blueberries

DIRECTIONS:
Preheat oven to 350° Fahrenheit.
In a large bowl, beat together the
butter, coconut oil, and sugar for 3
minutes. In a separate bowl, combine
the salt, baking soda, almond and
tapioca flours, and cinnamon. After
three minutes, add each egg into the
butter mixture one at a time, fully
combining each egg before adding
the next. Then slowly add in the flour
mixture until combined and beat
for two more minutes. Fold in the
blueberries and lemon zest and add
to 8x8 pan. Bake for 65-77 minutes.
Remove the pan from the oven. Let it
cool and enjoy!

Cooking Time: 65-77 Minutes

Serving Size: 15

Cooking Appliance: Oven

Notes:

187

Vegan Raspberry Bars

INGREDIENTS:
1 yellow cake mix
2 1/2 cups quick-cooking oats
1 3/4 sticks Miyoko's vegan butter
13 oz jar raspberry preserves

DIRECTIONS:
Preheat oven to 350° Fahrenheit.
Add cake mix, oats, and vegan
butter to a bowl and mix
until it becomes a crumble. Take 1/2
crumble and press into the bottom
of a 9x13 pan. Spread raspberry
preserves on the crumble in the
pan. Leave a 1/2" border around
the edges of the pan without
preserves. Sprinkle remaining
crumble on top of the preserves
and smash it down. Place in the
oven for 30 minutes and wait until
it has cooled to enjoy!

Recipe inspired by Sue Snyder.

Cooking Time: 30 Minutes

Serving Size: 30

Cooking Appliance: Oven

Notes:

Zucchini Banana Bread

INGREDIENTS:
2 zucchinis
2 bananas, mashed
1/3 cup chocolate chips
1/4 cup coconut oil, melted
1/4 cup coconut sugar
2 eggs
1/4 cup maple syrup
1/2 teaspoon baking soda
1/2 teaspoon baking powder
1 teaspoon cinnamon
1 teaspoon vanilla
1/2 teaspoon salt
2 cups all-purpose flour
2 tablespoons pecans, chopped (optional)

DIRECTIONS:
Preheat oven to 350° Fahrenheit.
Grate two zucchinis and squeeze out excess water with a strainer then set aside. In a large bowl, whisk together banana, coconut sugar, maple syrup, melted coconut oil, eggs, and vanilla. Then add the all-purpose flour, cinnamon, baking soda, baking powder, salt and whisk for 1 minute. Now fold in the zucchini and chocolate chips using a spatula. Grease a 9x5 inch glass loaf pan with oil and pour in the batter. Top batter with the chopped nuts and extra banana slices. Place the bread in the oven for 65-70 minutes, covering the loaf after 40 minutes to prevent the sides from burning. I know its hard, but wait 1 hour before cutting into the loaf and enjoy!

Cooking Time: 65-70 Minutes

Serving Size: 12

Cooking Appliance: Oven

Notes:

Adam's Amazing Carrot Cake

INGREDIENTS:
2 1/3 cups sifted all-purpose flour
(sifted, then measured)
1 cup sweetened flaked coconut
1 tablespoon cinnamon
1/4 teaspoon ginger
2 1/2 teaspoons baking powder
1 teaspoon salt
1/2 teaspoon baking soda
2 cups sugar
1/2 cup avocado oil
1/2 cup unsweetened applesauce
4 large eggs
2 teaspoons vanilla extract
2 cups finely grated peeled carrots
1 - 20 oz can crushed pineapple, very well drained
1/2 cup ground walnuts (optional)

FROSTING INGREDIENTS:
½ cup (1 stick) unsalted butter, softened
8 oz cream cheese, softened (brick-style, not spreadable)
1 teaspoon vanilla extract
¼ teaspoon salt
4 cups powdered sugar

DIRECTIONS:
Preheat the oven to 350°F. Butter and parchment three 9" diameter cake pans with 1 1/2" high sides (8" works, too - cake layers will be taller and take slightly longer to bake). Combine 1/3 cup flour with coconut in a food processor. Process until slightly chopped. Add grated carrots and pulse until finer in texture. Whisk remaining 2 cups flour, cinnamon, ginger, baking powder, salt, and baking soda in a bowl to blend. Using an electric mixer, beat sugar, oil, and applesauce in a large bowl to blend. Add eggs 1 at a time, beating well after each addition. Beat in vanilla. Beat in flour-spice mixture. Stir in coconut-carrot mixture and crushed pineapple. Add walnuts if using. Divide batter among pans. Bake until a tester inserted into the center of the cakes comes out clean, about 30 minutes. Cool in pans on racks for 1 hour. Run a knife around the edge of pans to loosen cakes. Turn cakes out onto racks; cool completely. Frost and stack!

Cooking Time: 30 Minutes

Serving Size: 20

Cooking Appliance: Oven

Notes:

Recipe inspired by Adam Beeman.

Banana Cake

INGREDIENTS:
1 gluten-free yellow cake mix
3 ripe bananas, mashed
1 teaspoon cinnamon
1 teaspoon baking soda
1/2 cup cold water
2 eggs
3/4 cup avocado oil

ICING:
1/2 cup Miyoko's Vegan Butter, melted
1/4 cup almond milk
1/4 cup coconut sugar or
golden monk fruit sweetener
2 cups organic powdered sugar

DIRECTIONS:
Preheat oven to 350° Fahrenheit.
Add all the cake batter ingredients
to a bowl and mix to combine.
Grease a 9x13 inch glass pan, then place
parchment on top. Pour batter into
pan, place in the oven, and bake for 30
minutes.

ICING DIRECTIONS:
In a sauce pan, melt the butter
with coconut sugar and milk, stirring
constantly and bring this mixture to
a boil. Take off the stove and let cool
for 7-10 minutes. Add in the powdered
sugar, whisking constantly until
combined. Pour the warm mixture over
the cake and let cool completely. Enjoy!

Cooking Time: 30-40 Minutes

Serving Size: 20

Cooking Appliance: Oven

Notes:

Recipe inspired by Pam Spring Feldeisen.

Cherry Crumble

INGREDIENTS:
Crust Ingredients:
2 cups quick-cooking oats
2 cups almond flour
1 1/4 cups brown sugar
2 sticks of vegan butter, melted
Filling Ingredients:
8 cups cherries, pitted
1/2 cup coconut sugar
6 tablespoons lemon juice
1/2 cup corn starch
1 teaspoon cinnamon

DIRECTIONS:
Preheat oven to 375° Fahrenheit. Then combine the crust ingredients in a bowl and mix until fully combined. In 13x9 dish, press half the crumb mixture into the bottom and place in the oven for 12 minutes or until golden. While the crust is cooking add all the filling ingredients to a large pot and cook for 10-15 minutes or until the mixture has thickned. Make sure to smash the cherries in the pot. Once the crust is cooked, add the prepared filling to the dish and top with the rest of the crust. Cook for 20-25 minutes or until the crust is golden brown and the cherries are bubbling. Let cool then serve and enjoy!
Vegan Recipe

Cooking Time: 20-25 Minutes

Serving Size: 20

Cooking Appliance: Oven & Stove

Notes:

Baked
Apple Delight

INGREDIENTS:
2 apples
2 teaspoons cinnamon
8 tablespoons water

DIRECTIONS:
Preheat oven to 350° Fahrenheit.
Chop your apple into 6 large slices.
Carefully using a mandoline
thinly slice the apples. Add to a
bowl with the cinnamon and mix
until coated. Using a muffin tin
arrange your apple in the shape
of a rose. Each apple should make
3-4 roses. Add 1 tablespoon water
to each apple muffin tin and place
in the oven for 30 minutes until
the apples have softened. Once
removed from the oven eat
Immediately. You can enjoy these
alone or paired with your favorite
ice cream.

Vegan Recipe

Cooking Time: 30 Minutes

Serving Size: 2

Cooking Appliance: Oven

Notes:

The Granola

INGREDIENTS:
4 cups rolled organic oats
2 cups unsweetened shaved coconut
1 cup organic ground flax seeds
1 cup pecan pieces
1 cup unsalted pumpkin seeds or almonds
1/4 cup egg whites
2 teaspoons cinnamon
1/2 cup avocado or coconut oil
1/4 cup maple syrup
1 teaspoon vanilla
2 1/2 tablespoons melted honey

DIRECTIONS:
Preheat oven to 250° Fahrenheit. In a large bowl, add the oats, coconut, flax seeds, pecans, egg whites, and cinnamon. Next in a sauce pan, add the oil, maple syrup, and vanilla and heat for 5 minutes. Pour the wet ingredients into the dry ingredients and mix to combine. Add the mixture to 2 large parchment-lined baking sheets. Bake for 50 minutes, stirring after 20 minutes. When there are 10 minutes left, drizzle the melted honey over the mixture and stir again. Bake remaining 10 minutes. Cool completely. Place in an airtight container and enjoy!

Recipe inspired by Gina Walsh and Traci Coffman.

Cooking Time: 50 minutes

Serving Size: 20

Cooking Appliance: Oven & Stove

Notes:

thank you

Thank you Thania Diaz and Donna Bronkema for teaching me how to properly edit and design my cookbook.
Thank you Cindie Baker, Mary Patton, and Stacey Marsh for all your hours of proofreading.